HEROES AND WARRIORS

Tecumseh

VISIONARY CHIEF OF THE SHAWNEE

JASON HOOK
Plates by RICHARD HOOK

91-63

Firebird Books

Acknowledgements

Many thanks to Badger and Dawn Kirby; Mike Johnson. Also to Ellen Jamieson at the Heye Foundation's Museum of the American Indian.

First published in the UK 1989 by Firebird Books
P.O. Box 327, Poole, Dorset BH15 2RG

Copyright © 1989 Firebird Books Ltd
Text copyright © 1989 Jason Hook

Distributed in the United States by
Sterling Publishing Co, Inc,
387 Park Avenue South, New York, NY 10016–8810

Distributed in Australia by
Capricorn Link (Australia) Pty Ltd
PO Box 665, Lane Cove, NSW 2066

British Library Cataloguing in Publication Data

Hook, Jason
   Tecumseh: visionary chief of the Shawnee. ——— (Heroes and warriors).
   1. Shawnee. Chiefs. Tecumseh, 1768–1813
   I. Title II. Series
   970.004'97
   ISBN 1 85314 012 0   (paperback)
   ISBN 1 85314 024 4   (cased)

Series editor Stuart Booth
Designed by Kathryn S.A. Booth
Typeset by Inforum Typesetting, Portsmouth
Monochrome origination by Castle Graphics, Frome
Colour separations by Kingfisher Facsimile
Colour printed by Barwell Colour Print (Midsomer Norton)
Printed and bound in Great Britain by The Bath Press

Tecumseh

VISIONARY CHIEF OF THE SHAWNEE

Portrait of Tecumseh by Benjamin J. Lossing from about 1875. Lossing based the head upon a pencil sketch made from life at Vincennes in 1808 by a young French fur trader named Pierre Le Dru. Of Tecumseh's dress in the sketch, Lossing noted, 'he appears as a brigadier-general of the British army, and is from a rough drawing, which I saw in Montreal in the summer of 1858, made at Malden soon after the surrender of Detroit . . . When in full dress he wore a cocked hat and plume, but would not give up his blue breech-cloth, red leggings fringed with buckskin, and buckskin moccasins.' Note also the three small crosses suspended from the cartilage of Tecumseh's nose, and his George III peace medal, apparently inherited from an ancestor.

TECUMSEH'S 'OLD NORTHWEST'

But hear me: a single twig breaks, but the bundle of sticks is strong. Someday I will embrace our brother tribes and draw them into a bundle and together we will win our country back from the whites.

(Tecumseh speaking of the Greenville Treaty of 1795)

Uncommon Genius

As the fledgling European settlements in the North-east of North America grew in size, friendly contact with the native Americans inevitably dissolved into a bitter dispute for land. Among the tribes of the eastern Woodlands, and of the Old Northwest of settled America, there were a succession of Indian leaders with the vision and influence to unite the scattered tribes in concerted defence. Metacom of the Wampanoags, known to the whites as King Philip, forged the first great Indian alliance in 1675. Almost a century later, the Ottawa leader Pontiac again welded a number of Woodlands tribes together in a brief repulsion of the white man's burgeoning civilisation.

The Woodlands culture region.

No Indian, though, attempted to unite the tribes on the scale visualized by Tecumseh, the Shawnee chief and visionary. Repudiating tribal rivalries, Tecumseh conceived the Indians as a distinct people, not as a succession of divided nations. He attempted to unite not merely a few select tribes, but all the eastern Indians from Canada to the deep south. He denied any right of the whites to purchase land from whichever tribe would sell it, and insisted upon common ownership by all the Indians. By pursuing passionately his grand vision – that of a single Indian confederacy and even an American Indian state – Tecumseh embodied the eastern Indians' last hope of saving their culture.

His breadth of vision, the eloquence with which he recruited tribes to his cause, and his constant humanity towards his enemies earned him great respect from the Indians and whites alike. He is often spoken of as the greatest of all the remarkable chiefs to have emerged during the long struggle of the Indian Wars. One of his fiercest adversaries said of him:

The implicit obedience and respect which followers of Tecumseh pay him is really astonishing and more than any other circumstance bespeaks him one of those uncommon geniuses which spring up occasionally to produce revolutions and overturn the established order of things. If it were not for the vicinity of the United States, he would perhaps be the founder of an Empire that would rival in glory Mexico or Peru.

(General William Harrison)

The Shawnee

It is impossible to assign a specific location to the Shawnee, since they were among the most fragmented of tribes and moved to new areas with great frequency. Their name means 'southerners' and they demonstrated aspects of both Eastern and South-eastern Indian cultures.

Migration and Conflict

The Shawnee were first documented living in the Ohio Valley. Between 1662 and 1673, they were ousted from their homeland by frequent attacks from the powerful Iroquois tribes. In order to survive, the Shawnee split into a number of fragments, probably based on their five hinterland divisions; and scattered in various directions.

The history of Shawnee migrations in the 1600s is complex and obscure, but becomes clearer by the eighteenth century. A number of groups settled among the Delaware and Susquehannock tribes in Pennsylvania which became the major Shawnee territory in the early 1700s. They continued to live in the shadow of the powerful and dominant Iroquois. A second group established a permanent town among the Creek, first on the Chattahoochee River and later on the Tallapoosa River.

Iroquois intimidation and French promise of protection urged the Pennsylvania Shawnee westward; by 1731 some twelve hundred tribesmen occupied the Ohio headwaters. In 1735, the Hathawekela division precipitated a new series of complex migrations by taking flight after the killing of an Iroquois chief. Lower Shawnee Town was established on the Scioto before 1739, and by 1752 had become the tribal centre. The Shawnee were subsequently caught up in the French and British dispute for the Ohio Valley. The British treated them with contempt, and following General Braddock's defeat in 1755, they joined the victorious French. The Shawnee attacked frontier settlements in Pennsylvania and Virginia until the fall of Fort Duquesne restored the British presence in 1758. They then fought as allies of the British in the later years of the French and Indian Wars (1754–1763).

As the war drew to a close, the removal of the French threat opened the floodgates for settlers to invade the Kentucky and Ohio hunting grounds of the Shawnee. Also resentful of their mistreatment at the hands of the British, they joined the Indian uprising inspired by Pontiac in 1763. Following Pontiac's defeat, and the subsequent decline of the stabilising power of the Iroquois, the Shawnee faced open conflict with the settlers.

Tribe and Season

The Shawnee were divided into five patrilineal divisions, each traditionally having distinct political and ritual responsibilities. The Chillicothe (First Men) and Hathawekela (Eagle), each considered superior in power to the other divisions, were responsible for political affairs and

The cheaply-constructed, light but sturdy, smooth-bore, Northwest Guns enjoyed great popularity among the Indians, and were traded in vast quantities by the Hudson's Bay Company after 1750. With a large trigger guard to facilitate use by a mittened hand, and a distinctive serpent side-plate opposite the lock, the Northwest Gun was an impressive shock weapon at close range.

6

Beaded bag, typical of the Woodlands culture, attributed to Chief Tuskina of the Creek.

were expected to provide the tribal chief. The Mequachake (Red Earth) were responsible for medicine and health, and provided the priesthood. Tribal council and ritual were governed by the Piqua (Rising from Ashes) people. The Kishpokotha, a name of uncertain derivation, were Tecumseh's people; they were the war division of the Shawnee. The tribe was also divided into sub-groups according to the geographic location of its towns. These were related to the five divisions, since a town's chief was usually drawn from the division with the largest representation.

Each division had a peace chief and a war chief who made decisions, affecting all the Shawnee people, in a council that was advised by elders and presided over by the tribal chief. Chieftainship was often hereditary, though powerful men would naturally rise to influence regardless of their birthright.

Shawnee economy combined hunting, gathering and the raising of crops, and became strongly orientated towards the fur trade after the

7

early 1700s. A Shawnee town was built around a large council house, which was surrounded by bark-covered lodges resembling the longhouses of the Iroquois. To the south lay the town's fields, which were planted with corn and beans in April. This was accomplished by the women, who also gathered wild plants, while the men occasionally fished or hunted for deer. After the final harvest in August, all but the elderly and infirm left the town and made their way slowly towards their winter camp, situated in a sheltered valley. There, the men undertook the vital winter hunt, securing deer, buffalo, bears, wild turkeys and other game. From December to February they turned their attention to trapping small animals, particularly the racoon. Then, in March, the Shawnee returned to their summer towns, and the cycle began again.

Warfare and Weapons

When the civil and war chiefs councilled for war against a certain tribe, a tomahawk painted with red clay was circulated through the towns of the Shawnee and their allies. The war medicine of the Kishpokotha traditionally accompanied a war party, whose departure was preceded by a war dance. The killing of twelve deer was ceremonially undertaken immediately prior to the warriors attacking their enemy.

If the warriors returned triumphant, they recited their honours at the War Dance, before undergoing a four-day period of purification in the council lodge. Prisoners, painted black, were condemned to death, unless first claimed by the principal female peace chief. Captives were forced to 'run the gauntlet' between two lines of armed men and women; they suffered torture and were often burned to death. Seemingly, there existed a religiously motivated cannibal society, headed by four old hags, and whose members burned and devoured the warriors' prisoners. More fortunate captives were adopted into the tribe.

Traditional Woodland weapons were the bow and stone-tipped arrow, used silently at long range from the forest's excellent concealment. The stone tomahawk and war club were used for hand-to-hand fighting.

Wood was very plentiful and most warriors were adept at fashioning it into ferocious war clubs. The most typical form was the ball-headed club, carved from ironwood to resemble a human hand or animal claw clasping a round ball. Some two feet in length with protective medicine symbols carved into the handles, these smoothly finished clubs made formidable weapons.

By 1763, the French trading posts, and more increasingly those of the British, had radically altered the Woodland Indians' armoury. Bows were largely replaced by guns, available from Montreal traders in exchange for twenty beaver skins. Iron knives facilitated the carving of wooden clubs, but these were rapidly replaced by gun-stock clubs mounted with vicious metal blades, and by iron-headed tomahawks.

Hudson Bay

Micmac

Algonquin

Abenaki

Ojibwa

L. Superior

Nipissing

Mohawk
Oneida

Pequot
Mahican

Ottawa

Huron

Wampanoag

Potawatomi

Narragasot

Menominee

Neutral

Delaware

Sauk

Seneca
Cayuga
Onondaga

Fox

Winnebago

L. Michigan

Kickapoo

Nanticoke

Miami

Shawnee

Susquehannock

North Atlantic Ocean

Illinois

*Major tribes of the North-east
culture area – Tecumseh's 'Old
Northwest'.*

9

Shawnee warriors often carried special sashes, with which to secure captive prisoners about their necks. These ties were also decorated with medicine symbols, and were believed to give supernatural assistance in taking captives. Armour, used by some Woodland tribes, was not typically worn by Shawnee warriors. Instead, the Shawnee relied upon medicines and amulets such as herbs, animal skins and the feathers of birds to invoke supernatural protection.

Woodlands Welfare

The Shawnee believed that their welfare and indeed their universe was wrapped up in the 'sacred packs'. Each of the five divisions originally possessed one of these tribal bundles; buckskin cases containing various amulets and medicine symbols. Their sanctity was such that they were kept in separate lodges, treated like humans, and regularly shifted to ensure their comfort. Few spoke of them, to avoid desecrating their medicine.

The bundles were given to the Shawnee by Our Grandmother, the most prominent Shawnee deity. She created the Earth, and taught the Shawnee how to live. Through the bundles, She continued to control her children; and the bundles also provided the most sacred path to Her. Both the sacred packs and Our Grandmother were aspects of the ceremonial dances through which communal worship was made. The most important of these were the Spring and Fall Bread Dances. In these, twelve women (twelve being considered the sacred number) cooked meat, secured by twelve hunters, for a ceremonial feast; prayers and ceremonies were offered in a plea for plentiful game.

Shooting Star

Tecumseh was born in March 1768, at the Shawnee village of Piqua, on Mad River, about six miles south-west of present day Springfield, Ohio. His father was a Shawnee warrior named Puckeshinwa, which meant 'I alight from flying' or 'One who drops down'. Puckeshinwa's first wife had been a Creek Indian, but Tecumseh's mother was a Shawnee woman from among the Creeks. Called Methoataske, her name signified 'Turtle laying eggs in the sand.'

Puckeshinwa and Methoataske's first child, a son named Cheesekau, had been born while the couple were living with a Shawnee group among the Creeks of eastern Alabama. Then, as these Shawnee migrated north, they had a daughter, Menewaulaakoosee, and another son, Sauawaseekau.

There are two versions of the circumstances of Tecumseh's birth. The first states that Tecumseh was born one of triplets. One of the three was deformed and died young. The other was called Laulewasika, and was destined to gain great fame under the name of 'the Prophet'. The second and more likely version states that Tecumseh alone was born in 1768, while the Prophet, possibly one of twins, was born three years later. A fifth son, Nehaaseemo, was born in the intervening years, and a seventh, Kumskaukau some time later.

Methoataske gave birth to Tecumseh in a hut specially erected near to the family's lodge. Mother and son stayed in the hut for ten days before the child's naming ceremony was held. At a feast given for the parents'

An early depiction of Tecumseh from an unidentified relief cut – thought to be after an original by Trenchard, after Bortram.

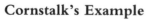

A conical lodge, covered with bark, used alongside the domed wigwam and substantial longhouse as a home in the Eastern Woodlands.

relatives, an old man named the boy Tecumseh (or Tekumthe) meaning 'Flying or Springing Across'. This, like his father's name, signified membership of the Great Lynx Clan, one of the patrilineal clans of the Shawnee. The name Tecumseh was consequently translated as 'Crouching Lynx', or 'Panther', or 'Shooting Star', the Shawnee equating a meteor with a springing lynx. Members of the Great Lynx clan were responsible for guarding the rear of a returning war-party, the most dangerous position.

From his father, Tecumseh also inherited a place in the Kishpokotha division of the Shawnee. Responsible for warfare, this group were 'always inclined to war and gave much trouble to the nation'. The war chief of the tribe was expected to be a member of both the Great Lynx Clan and the Kishpokotha division. Clearly, Tecumseh's very lineage directed his life towards war.

Cornstalk's Example

Though the Royal Proclamation of 1763 had prohibited white settlement west of the Appalachians, the Iroquois ceded Kentucky to settlers in the year of Tecumseh's birth. Virginia's colonial governor, the Earl of Dunmore, granted Shawnee land to veterans of the French and Indian Wars, and there were growing clashes as the Shawnee defended their hunting grounds. In 1774, frontiersmen brutally murdered thirteen Shawnee and Mingo (displaced Iroquois tribesmen) in a series of unprovoked attacks. The victims' relatives formed a war-party which killed an equivalent number of settlers, though the Shawnee, unable to secure allies, refrained from formally going to war.

This attack, though, precipitated Lord Dunmore's War. A militia of 1500 men marched from Virginia and destroyed a Shawnee town in the Muskingum Valley. The Shawnee appealed to the Iroquois League for help but only the Seneca chief Logan rallied to their cause. While

Iroquois pipe-tomahawk, symbol of both peace and war.

12

Dunmore led another force from Fort Pitt, Pittsburgh, Andrew Lewis led a column through the Kanawha Valley. In an attempt to defend the Scioto Valley, the Shawnee, led by the chief Cornstalk, made a surprise dawn attack on Lewis' force at Point Pleasant on 6th October 1774. The battle raged throughout the day, and the Virginians lost 50 dead and 100 wounded before the Shawnee succumbed. Tecumseh's father Puckeshinwa and eldest brother Cheesekau, fought courageously and survived the battle of Point Pleasant.

In November, Cornstalk met Lord Dunmore at Chillicothe, and signed a treaty of peace. He recognised the Ohio River as the southern boundary of Shawnee territory, leaving Kentucky open to settlement. Cornstalk received great recognition for his generalship at the Battle of Point Pleasant. He also demonstrated his outstanding ability as an orator when appeasing those tribal factions that opposed the treaty. The young Tecumseh regarded Cornstalk with awe, and would himself demonstrate the same qualities in later life.

While Cornstalk diligently enforced the treaty, the white settlers disregarded it and continued to invade the Shawnee lands in Ohio. That year, a party of frontiersmen surprised Puckeshinwa in the woodlands near the Piqua settlement, and shot Tecumseh's father dead. His body was apparently found by Tecumseh and his mother, Methoataske, who instructed her young son to become a warrior like his father: 'a fire spreading over the hill and valley, consuming the race of dark souls.'

Such incidents drove the Shawnee towards war, and in 1777, Cornstalk took his son to Point Pleasant, to warn the settlers of the unrest. The chief and his son were taken prisoner, and shortly afterwards were murdered by soldiers in retaliation for the killing of a white settler. The Shawnee would seek vengeance for this outrage in a war that lasted nearly twenty years.

Tecumseh was adopted by Blackfish, leading chief of the main Shawnee settlement, Chillicothe. Having seen the white men cut down his father and Cornstalk, Tecumseh travelled between the Chillicothe and Piqua settlements, learning the lore of his people.

An Eastern Woodlands pipe-tomahawk, with engraving commemorating the killing of a European.

Cowardice and Courage

The Shawnee were inevitably drawn into the border wars of the American Revolution (1775–83). Even the peace faction joined the war against the settlers after the murder of Cornstalk; and alliance with the British simply furnished them with arms. American settlements came under frequent attacks from the start of the Revolution, and in 1776 the Shawnee joined a delegation of Delaware and Mohawks in recruiting Cherokee, Creek, Choctaw and Chickasaw to the British side. Tecumseh was to turn to these southern tribes when he sought support for his own wars some years later.

In 1778, the American general Edward Hand led a force from Fort Pitt

13

Typical Shawnee bead necklace. Like all such artefacts, its function was religious and decorative.

which destroyed Shawnee villages as far north as the Sandusky River. Major George Roger Clark's army of Kentuckians and Virginians also seized a number of Indian villages on the Ohio, and in 1780 destroyed the Chillicothe and Piqua settlements. The legendary frontiersman Daniel Boone had been captured with twenty-six other whites when Blackfish attacked Kentucky settlements in 1778. He was imprisoned at Chillicothe but later escaped his Shawnee captors. Also in 1780, a large number of Shawnee warriors joined loyalist Colonel William Byrd's 1000-strong Indian army in destroying the Kentucky settlements of Ruddle's and Martin's Stations, inflicting a heavy defeat on a force of Kentucky militia.

The destruction of their villages caused further migrations among the Shawnee. One group, the Hathawekela, travelled south to avoid conflict with the Americans, settling among the Creek possibly as early as 1774. Another group, primarily made up of the Kishpokotha and Piqua, migrated westward to escape the hostilities in 1780. Eventually, they settled in Missouri between the Mississippi and Whitewater Rivers, in Spanish territory. Tecumseh's mother, Methoataske, is believed to have travelled with this group. Tecumseh was left in the care of his brother Cheesekau, and remained with the Ohio Shawnee who rebuilt the Piqua settlement on the Miami River. Even this slight migration reflected the way in which American settlement was pushing the tribes ever westward.

Before he was thirteen, Tecumseh was probably sent out into the woodlands to seek a vision of supernatural assistance from some sacred helper. A Shawnee boy undertook this vision quest at an unusually early age compared with the other central Algonquin tribes, sometimes as young as seven years old. With his face blackened by charcoal, the vision-seeker fasted alone for up to four days, watching for some indication of his sacred power or 'medicine'. It is known that Tecumseh received a vision of the Buffalo, which procured him a powerful war medicine.

As a boy, Tecumseh distinguished himself in his early training as a warrior, and took responsibility for arranging his comrades into sides for sham battles. His courage and vigilance are said to have been keenly developed at an early age. When he was first tested in real warfare, though, Tecumseh was found severely wanting. At the age of fifteen, in 1783, he joined Cheesekau in a skirmish on the banks of the Mad River. When the engagement began, and blood started flowing, Tecumseh turned tail and ran. That night he lay in his lodge thoroughly ashamed of his cowardice. The momentary weakness, though, steeled rather than broke him, and Tecumseh would never again run from an enemy.

The Treaty of Paris in 1783 made no provision for the Indian population. As the British withdrew from along the Ohio, the Shawnee continued to clash with the settlers in the Old Northwest. The numerous tribes of the Ohio country held a great council on the Sandusky in 1783, and formed an Indian confederacy to 'defend their country against all invaders'. They took up arms to protect their boundary on the Ohio River, attacking the supply boats that navigated its waters and the wagon trains moving west from Fort Pitt.

Tecumseh overcame his earlier indiscretion and participated boldly in the Shawnee attacks which imperilled every flatboat that carried settlers down the Ohio from Pennsylvania. When aged about seventeen, he showed great prowess in one such attack, which took place above present day Maysville. All the settlers were killed except one, who was taken prisoner. The captive of Tecumseh's war-party was painted black and detained in the village for one night. The following day, he was tied by a vine to a white oak sapling, and the warriors tortured him to death with burning brands. Tecumseh, a silent spectator, was horrified by the inhumanity of the act; he considered it dishonourable to the name of a warrior and simply barbaric in content. Rather than brooding on the matter, Tecumseh expressed his views to the other warriors with such eloquence and passion that they resolved to abandon the practice. The fact that the Shawnee adhered to this promise, refraining thereafter from burning captives, bears testimony to the prodigious powers of oration possessed already by the seventeen-year-old Tecumseh. He continued to display the same humanity and compassion throughout his life, his standing among the whites being greatly enhanced when he saved a number of white prisoners from torture and death.

Shawnee tomahawk with pierced design and decoration of trade tacks and blue cloth.

Little Turtle's War

By the age of twenty, Tecumseh had risen to a position of prominence among his people, leading many war-parties against the Americans. He continued to show great bravery in battle, and on one occasion escaped a seemingly impossible situation with a masterly charge, cutting his way through the ranks of Americans that surrounded him.

One autumn, possibly in 1788, Tecumseh participated in a buffalo hunt, and was thrown from his horse. He suffered a severely broken thigh, which left him with a shortened, disfigured leg, and a limp when walking. Slowly recovering the following spring, but finding himself unable to keep pace with a war-party, Tecumseh apparently despaired of becoming a successful warrior and hunter to the extent of once trying to kill himself.

About 1789, Tecumseh made the first of the many journeys that were to elevate him above the tribal and clanship rivalries and that so distinguished his life. Still recovering from his leg injury, he joined Cheesekau in riding to his mother's Shawnee village in Missouri. He also visited the

Powder-horn of white manufacture, with brass and wood fittings, attached by leather thong to a finger-woven woollen sash; from the Great Lakes region around 1780. The Great Lakes Indians had woven sashes of hemp and animal hair since prehistoric times and readily adapted the technique to the white man's coloured yarns.

Shawnee of southern Illinois and the Miami tribe in Indiana. Later in the year, together with Cheesekau and their mother, Tecumseh joined a party of Kickapoo Indians travelling south to join the Creek and Cherokee. Having fully recovered from his fall, Tecumseh joined the Creek in fighting American settlers, before returning north.

Cheesekau was killed by white men in a skirmish on the Tennessee frontier in 1789, and Tecumseh bitterly answered the call of the Miami chief Michikinikwa – Little Turtle – to unite against the Americans. President George Washington had ordered General Josiah Harmar to lead an expedition to pacify the Old Northwest, and Little Turtle raised a force of Miami, Shawnee, Potawatomi, and Chippewa to meet him. Little Turtle was supported by Blue Jacket of the Shawnee and Buckongahelas, a Delaware chief. In 1790, Harmar, a heavy-drinking, ill-disciplined general, led 1400 men – 1100 of them being militia – north from Fort Washington, Cincinnati. Little Turtle, an astute commander, retreated slowly up the Maumee valley, burning the occasional village to feign a desperate rout. In September, with Harmar drawn deep into the woodlands, the Indians turned and outflanked the disorganised Americans. Tecumseh joined the two ambushes which saw 183 soldiers killed and 31 wounded. Harmar retreated, claiming a victory, while Little Turtle watched him go.

Routing the Militia

A new American expedition was organised in March 1791, comprising about 2000 men, again largely militia purchased 'from prisons, wheelbarrows and brothels at two dollars a month.' It was led by General Arthur St. Clair, Governor of the North-West Territory and a hero of the American Revolution. Like Harmar, St. Clair had no experience of fighting Indians. As he led his men towards the Miami and Wabash Rivers, Tecumseh's scouts harried his flanks and reported his movements. St. Clair was suffering so severely from gout that he had to be borne on a litter. His 600 regular soldiers had to guard the supply train from the ill-fed militia; by November, some 600 men had deserted.

Reaching high ground on the upper Wabash on 3rd November, St. Clair relaxed his defences – and the following dawn, Little Turtle struck. Emerging silently and suddenly from the forest with Tecumseh at their head, the Indians routed the outlying militia men, and attacked St. Clair's artillery. With smoke choking the air, St. Clair mounted several bayonet charges; but the Indians simply melted back into the woodlands and picked off the greenhorn troops.

Completely surrounded, and with half his men dead, St. Clair ordered the retreat, battling through the Indian lines to effect it. The Indians pursued the army for four miles, but the rout continued clear to Fort Jefferson, twenty-nine miles away, with many men discarding their guns. Tecumseh had been a prominent figure in this, the worst ever

Tecumseh, wearing Kishpokotha war-bundle split feather plumes, with his face blackened for war, harangues 5000 Indians at the Creek town of Tukabatchi, October 1811, seeking to weld together his confederacy.

disaster suffered by the Americans in the Indian Wars; 630 soldiers were killed and a further three hundred wounded. Not surprisingly, settlement of the Old Northwest slowed to a cautious trickle.

Tecumseh continued to harass any who dared to settle on his lands. In May, 1792, he led an attack against the family of John Waggoner. Waggoner outran the limping chief, but his wife was killed and their children captured and adopted into the Shawnee tribe. Shortly afterwards, a party of twenty-eight whites led by renowned frontiersman Simon Kenton assailed a group of Shawnees led by Tecumseh. Though accompanied by only ten warriors, Tecumseh drove off the Americans after a ferocious fight.

Later in the year, Tecumseh again journeyed south, replacing his brother in the southern Shawnees, and leading their allies, the Creeks and Cherokee, against the settlements near Nashville. His reputation grew quickly among the tribes of the south-eastern states, and he formed many friendships upon which he could call in later life.

Fallen Timbers and the Greenville Treaty

Between the autumns of 1792 and 1793, the U.S. Army General-in-Chief 'Mad Anthony' Wayne drilled and disciplined a select force of over 3000 troops at Legionville and Washington. The Government made peace overtures to the Indians at the 1793 Sandusky Conference, but after the chiefs insisted upon recognition of the Ohio as their eastern boundary, Wayne took to the field.

Following St. Clair's route, Wayne first established Fort Recovery near Greenville, Ohio, and then Fort Adams at the mouth of the Auglaize in the summer of 1794. Little Turtle and Tecumseh led an attack against Fort Recovery, but it was repelled. Little Turtle shrewdly recognised the calibre of his new adversary and advised the Indians to seek peace with this 'chief who never sleeps'. Unheedingly, the warriors ousted him in favour of the less able Turkey Foot.

Wayne, whom the Indians called 'Black Snake', pursued the Indians north to the British post of Fort Miami, where the Indians rejected a new offer of peace. On 20th August 1794, Wayne led a surprise attack against the Indians at Fallen Timbers, on the Maumee River. Tecumseh's party of scouts met the initial charge of the infantry, and bore the brunt of the fiercest fighting. Tecumseh's courage was again outstanding and he continued to rally the Indians the width of the battlefield even after his rifle jammed. When the Indians were overwhelmed and thrown into retreat, Tecumseh led a small party in capturing a field-piece. They cut free the horses harnessed to the gun, and rode them to safety.

The Indians, most of whom carried British weapons, fled to Fort Miami; but the soldiers there, in fear of Wayne, refused to open the gates. Only 38 Americans fell in the fighting, while several hundred Indians including another of Tecumseh's brothers, were killed. Wayne laid

Knife and knife-sheath of the Eastern Great Lakes region, before 1800. The iron-bladed knife, a trade item, has a brass handle inlaid with tortoiseshell. Its elaborate leather sheath illustrates the intricacy of Woodland quillwork — dyed porcupine quills sewn with sinew — before the increased use of trade beads. The strap is also decorated with quills wrapped around leather thongs.

Tenskwatawa, clutching his 'medicine-fire', urges on Tecumseh's alliance of Woodlands warriors in the ill-fated assault upon General Harrison's militia at Tippecanoe, 3.45 a.m., 7th November 1811.

waste to the Indian villages before establishing Fort Wayne in Indiana at the confluence of the St. Joseph and St. Mary Rivers.

Wayne wintered at Greenville, where he called the tribes to council in the spring of 1795. A thousand Indians, with chiefs representing twelve different tribes, attended, and conferred for two months. On 3rd August, they signed the Greenville Treaty, ceding most of Ohio, a portion of Indiana, and more distant enclaves including Detroit, to the United States in exchange for annuities of $10,000. The treaty concluded the last throes of the Revolution and a Wyandot chief reflected that, 'we . . . acknowledge the fifteen United States . . . to be our father . . . (and) must call them brother no more.'

Blue Jacket signed for the Shawnee, and the Miami also accepted American rule as Little Turtle touched the pen. He declared: 'I am the last to sign it, and I will be the last to break it.' True to his word he remained a proponent of peace, and became a celebrity among the white settlers.

Tecumseh was furious with the chiefs, recognising that the treaty would simply open up the Northwest to ever greater settlement. He did not attend the council, and refused to accept its conclusions. Splitting with Blue Jacket, Tecumseh led a faction of warriors west to the Wabash drainage, and became the leading hostile chief in the region. He declared the Greenville Treaty worthless:

My heart is a stone: heavy with sadness for my people; cold with the knowledge that no treaty will keep the whites out of our lands; hard with the determination to resist as long as I live and breathe. Now we are weak and many of our people are afraid. But hear me: a single twig breaks, but the bundle of twigs is strong. Someday I will embrace our brother tribes and draw them into a bundle and together we will win our country back from the whites.

Rebecca Galloway

Finding support among the Delaware, Tecumseh resided in Indiana until about 1805. In 1796, he married a half-breed woman named Manete who bore him a son shortly before their quarrels caused her to leave. The boy was called Puchethei, meaning 'crouching or watching his prey', again signifying membership of the Great Medicine Lynx clan.

Just before the end of the eighteenth century, Tecumseh met and formed a close friendship with Rebecca Galloway, the beautiful blonde daughter of an Ohio farmer. They met frequently, and Rebecca taught her eager student to speak English fluently, and to read the Bible and great literary works such as Shakespeare. Tecumseh also learned World history, and Rebecca told him of the great white leaders of the past like Alexander the Great and Julius Caesar. Possibly in light of this new knowledge, he considered the attempts of Pontiac to unite the Indian tribes, and his plans for building an Indian confederacy matured. Rebecca's teaching also confirmed in Tecumseh's mind the belief that all Indians held common ownership of the land, and that no one tribe had the right to sell it.

This Northern Ojibwa-type knife and sheath of about 1800 demonstrates the Indians' fusion of European culture with their own. The horn-handled iron blade is held in a leather sheath lined with birch-bark, which is decorated with typical quillwork, horsehair fringes, glass beads, green wool, and brass cones.

18

The compassion for which Tecumseh was already famous, was enhanced by his relationships with the Galloway family. Rebecca was also naturally fascinated by Tecumseh's way of life, and, according to one tale, pressed the Shawnee chief on the medicinal effects of a certain flowering tree. Tecumseh purportedly told her:

The red man takes the powder of the flowers and leaves . . . into battle with him. If the bullet bites or the arrow pierces, the potion quiets the pain. If the warrior falls in battle, it eases him. What you had in your hand, the fruit, is best. With it, the pain of the fire at the stake is little. If wounded the warrior can be removed to a place of safety without pain. The powder is as powerful to quiet pain as your opium is, but does not do the harm it has done. No paleface knows its power. It is our secret.

(W.A. Galloway)

Tecumseh eventually proposed marriage to Rebecca, who, with her father's permission, consented on condition that Tecumseh abandoned his Indian ways and lived like a white man. For a month Tecumseh deliberated, before sadly leaving Rebecca, telling her that he could never abandon his people.

A Woodlands badger-skin medicine bag adorned with eagle talons, quills, beads, ribbons and bells, probably Ojibwa of about 1800. The badger was a protective spirit to the Midewiwin or Medicine Lodge Society. This was an esoteric priesthood, found among many of the Woodlands tribes, including Tecumseh's Shawnee, who possessed an occult knowledge of killing and curing. It was demonstrated at annual ceremonies, with the use of herbs, medicine bundles and the magical 'shooting' of a cowrie shell into the patient's body. The badger has been spiritually resurrected by the eagle talon 'horns'.

Buffalo and Bundle

A new threat to the Shawnee lands was meanwhile engendered by the formation in 1800 of Indiana Territory, creating political machinery for administering the land west of Ohio. General William Henry Harrison became Governor of Indiana, and was also given the rôle of Superintendent of Indian Affairs. As such, Harrison, an ambitious and capable administrator as well as a notable soldier, became a life-long adversary of Tecumseh.

About this time, Tecumseh received a new vision from his guardian spirit, the Buffalo, in which he was taught a sacred war dance. This Buffalo Dance is still performed by the Shawnee, and by the Delaware, among whom Tecumseh was living at this time. Participants invoke the Buffalo's power by painting a buffalo-head design on their chests, and a red line from the corner of each eye, and performing a simple dance imitating the buffalo's movements. The power of the dance was such that it was quickly adopted by the Shawnee and introduced to other tribes by Tecumseh during his later travels.

Tecumseh also became responsible for the sacred pack of the Kishpokotha Shawnee division, one of the five treasured, esoteric tribal bundles. The 'Tecumseh bundle' as it has become known, contained four plumes of hawk feathers; a wooden image of a man in Shawnee costume, with tiny bow and arrows; two turkey feather roach headdresses; and, according to myth, the flesh and bones of the Giant Horned Snake, a Shawnee deity. The bundle was opened for the tribal war ceremonies, and Tecumseh's possession of it reflects his standing in the tribe. He even added his own talisman to the pack, an ancient trefoil-

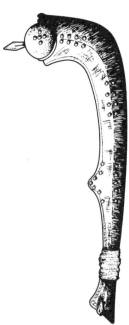

shaped steel tomahawk, which became an integral part of the bundle's ceremonies.

Tecumseh's medicine attained great renown, and one Winnebago informant remembered him as 'a powerful man. Bullets could not penetrate him, and indeed it was impossible to kill him in any way.'

The Prophet

During this period, contact with white civilisation had a further detrimental effect upon the Shawnee and other tribes of the region. Traders opened negotiations and bidded for trade by offering liberal quantities of whiskey, to which many Indians became wretchedly addicted. Tecumseh shrewdly preached abstinence, and Colonel John Johnston described him at the time:

Sober and abstencious; never indulging in the use of liquors, nor catering to excess; fluent in conversation, and a great public speaker. He despised dress, and all effeminacy of manners; he was disinterested, hospitable, generous and humane – the resolute indefatigable advocate of the rights and independence of the Indians.

Ball-headed club, adorned with brass tacks and wood spikes. This example from the Great Lakes, 1800–50.

One of the worst drunkards, though, was Tecumseh's brother, Laulewasika, a powerful man whose loss of one eye gave him a gruesome appearance. His name meant 'Rattle', and he was said to possess a belt which he could transform into a rattlesnake. Laulewasika was unpopular and feared as a young man, and Thomas Forsyth recalled of him: 'When a boy he was a perfect vagabond and as he grew up he would not hunt and became a great drunkard.'

In 1805, Laulewasika fell into a trance, and awoke claiming to have spoken with the supreme deity, the Master of Life. He changed his name to Tenskwatawa, meaning 'The Open Door'; and in November, at a tribal council at the ancient capital of Wapakoneta, Ohio, he pronounced himself the Prophet.

Tenskwatawa preached against the adoption of the white man's way of life, his tools, clothes and weapons. In particular he condemned the use of alcohol that had so corrupted his own early life. Tenskwatawa promised the return of divine favour if the Shawnees returned to their traditional way of life. He also, rather curiously, proscribed use of the medicine bundles, songs and dances that were such a prominent feature of Shawnee culture. While intended to combat evil witchcraft, this rule also encompassed the traditional medicines and ceremonies of the Indians, and therefore met with strong opposition. It did, though, provide a medium through which Tenskwatawa could challenge those who opposed the rest of his doctrines.

Amongst a people whose way of life was severely threatened by the encroaching white civilisation – and delivered by such a wily preacher –

Tenskwatawa's religion quickly became popular among the Shawnee and their neighbouring tribes. Like the Delaware Prophet of Pontiac's time, Tenskwatawa created a religious movement which could be harnessed by Tecumseh for his own needs. Tenskwatawa inspired the fanaticism and became the figurehead of a movement of which Tecumseh gradually assumed control.

After Wayne's victory, the Indians had been divided into small groups who fought sporadically and individually to halt the continued invasion of their lands. In 1805, Tecumseh took his followers to Greenville, Ohio. There, he attempted to use the revitalization movement of his brother to re-unify the tribes, on the very site of the treaty signing that had divided them.

Tenskwatawa, Open Door, the Shawnee 'Prophet', painted in Washington by Henry Inman around 1830. The costume and likeness are accurate, corresponding to George Catlin's portrait of the Prophet, and the ear-rings and nose ornament are typical Shawnee.

Medicine of Prophecy
Tenskwatawa inevitably accompanied his preaching with claims to be

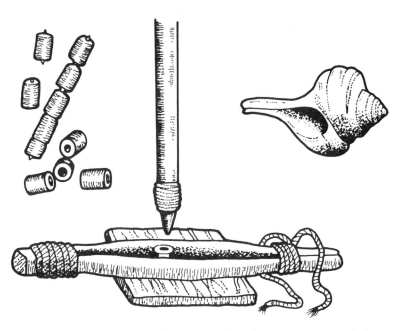

able to perform prophecy, healing and other supernatural feats. He travelled to distant tribes proclaiming his abilities, and teaching a ceremony closely related to the War Dance of Tecumseh. Amongst the Creek and Cherokee, followers of the Prophet anticipated a terrible hailstorm engulfing the whites and Indian unbelievers, from which Tenskwatawa would lead the faithful to safety. The Prophet also predicted that after four years, a blanket of darkness would cover the land, and the people's dead would be restored to them. He also foresaw the reappearance of plentiful game, in a doctrine with notable similarities to the Ghost Dance that would sweep the Plains in 1890.

As Tenskwatawa's popularity grew, and word of his abilities spread as far as the central Canadian Plains, Harrison attempted to quell the religious fervour. He told one tribe:

If he is really a prophet ask him to cause the sun to stand still, the moon to alter its course, the rivers to cease to flow, or the dead to rise from their graves. If he does these things you may then believe he has been sent from God.

The Prophet answered any doubts raised by Harrison, by calling a large assembly at Greenville and proclaiming that he would darken the face of the Sun. Shortly before noon, 16th June 1806, Tenskwatawa gestured triumphantly at the sky, as the sun was slowly eclipsed by the moon. 'Did I not speak the truth? See, the sun is dark!' he cried, as the Indians stared in terror at the sky and knew in their hearts that the Prophet must be holy.

The miracle of the eclipse spread Tenskwatawa's fame to the remotest tribes, from the Ottawa and Ojibwa, south to the Creek and Cherokee, and west as far as the Ponca, Mandan, Blackfoot and Sioux. Tenskwatawa and his agents travelled extensively to secure new disciples for his religion, and warriors for Tecumseh's wars. The Prophet carried sacred slabs, pictographic slats depicting his deities, which he presented to the war chiefs of the tribes. He also possessed a 'medicine fire' of feathers and beads to symbolise the 'eternal fire', an ancient Shawnee symbol. He called upon the Indians he visited to resurrect the tradition of maintaining an eternal fire in their lodge, and warned that should it die, they would die with it. Sacred strings of discoloured beans were also a prominent symbol of Tenskwatawa's medicine, and were said to contain the Prophet's own flesh. Tenskwatawa instructed his followers to swear their allegiance to him by running these beans through their hands, in a ceremony known as 'shaking hands with the prophet.'

Tenskwatawa's most striking medicine, though, was a life-size representation of a corpse, described in 1830 by George Catlin:

He carried with him into every wig-wam that he visited, the image of a dead person of the size of life; which was made ingeniously of some light material, and always kept concealed under bandages of thin white muslin cloths and not to be opened; of this he made great mystery, and got his recruits to swear by touching a sacred string of white beans, which he had attached to his neck or some other way secreted about him. In this way, by his extraordinary cunning, he had carried terror into the country as far as he went; and had actually enlisted some eight or ten thousand men, who were sworn to follow him home . . .

Tenskwatawa also supervised a more practical terrorising of the Indians, when his followers purged those who opposed the Prophet's teachings. In the spring of 1809, a Kickapoo man was denounced as a witch and burned to death for refusing to surrender his medicine bundle. Several Delaware suffered the same fate, as did Leatherlips, the Syandot *sachem* or chief. The bloodshed was eventually halted by the intervention of Tecumseh, who also encouraged the Indians to abandon those chiefs who were too friendly towards the Americans; but through peaceful methods.

Prophet's Town

Tecumseh now conceived the idea of welding the divided tribes into a mighty alliance, though which to defend their lands. Tenskwatawa later told Catlin that:

Tecumseh's plans were to embody all the Indian tribes in a grand confederacy, from the province of Mexico, to the Great Lakes, to unite their forces in an army that would be able to meet and drive back the white people, who were continually advancing on the Indian tribes, and forcing them from their lands towards the Rocky Mountains.

Tecumseh insisted that the land was held in common by all the Indians, and that no single tribe had the right to independently sell its hunting grounds. His brother's creed held practical value to Tecumseh, for he knew that only by abandoning trade for the Americans' guns, tools,

The carved otter — running across the top of this ball-headed club — was a frequent addition to such weapons invoking the Woodlands' warrior's supernatural guardian in battle.

23

cloths and whiskey could the Indians hope to protect their independence. As early as 1806, he formed a powerful alliance with Roundhead, the leader of the most war-like Wyandot warriors.

In 1808, Tecumseh and Tenskwatawa established a settlement called Prophet's Town at the confluence of the Wabash and Tippecanoe Rivers. Apparently, the Miami tribe resented this intrusion into their hunting grounds; many of their chiefs were killed by Tenskwatawa's followers. This reduced the Prophet's popularity, so that while the Americans regarded him as the leader of the movement, Tecumseh was gradually assuming control.

That same year, Tecumseh made the first of his epic journeys to address tribes throughout the Old Northwest and the South, from the head of the Missouri down to Florida. Many of the old chiefs resisted his call to arms, preferring to preserve the Greenville Treaty, but most of the young warriors were excited by his plans for an Indian confederacy. Tecumseh cajoled great crowds with his exceptional oratory, and spoke privately with those chiefs of greatest influence. To the west he gained support from the Sauk and Winnebago tribes. To the south Creeks, Cherokees and Seminoles found new heart in his flowing speeches. Returning north, Tecumseh tried in vain to gain the support of the powerful Iroquois. By 1810, a thousand warriors were gathered at Prophet's Town, drawn from the Shawnee, Kickapoo, Delaware, Potawatomi, Ottawa and Chippewa tribes.

Vincennes

Tecumseh returned to Prophet's Town to discover that Harrison, in his bid to secure Indiana's statehood, had persuaded a number of chiefs to sell more of the Indian land. Harrison had met the older representatives of the Delaware, Miami and Potawatomi tribes at Fort Wayne, in the summer of 1809. Plying them with alcohol and sweet words, he persuaded the chiefs to sign the Treaty of Fort Wayne. This ceded three million acres of land, extending in a sixty-mile strip up the Wabash from Vincennes, in exchange for $7000 and an annuity of $1750. Tenskwatawa had failed to oppose the treaty; but Tecumseh, on his return, was outraged. His claim that the land was the Indians' common property was justified in this case; the three signatory tribes had sold land to which they had no claim. He refused to recognise the treaty, and, in his fury, even threatened to kill the chiefs that had touched the pen.

When Harrison learned of the displeasure at Prophet's Town, he dispatched a messenger to Tenskwatawa, who he still believed to be the leader of the Indians there. It invited him to Vincennes, assuring him 'that any claims he might have to the lands which had been ceded, were

not affected by the treaty; that he might come to Vincennes and exhibit his pretensions, and if they were found to be valid, the land would be either given up, or an ample compensation made for it.'

Opening Speeches

In August of 1810, Tecumseh arrived at Vincennes at the head of four hundred warriors, much to the alarm of the Americans. One officer present described Tecumseh as, 'one of the finest men I have ever met – about six feet high, straight with large, fine features and altogether a daring, bold-looking fellow.'

On 12th August, Tecumseh and some forty warriors met Harrison in a large portico erected before the governor's house. Harrison approached Tecumseh, and told him, 'Your father requests you to take a chair.'

With great indignation, Tecumseh walked away and sat on the ground in the shade of some trees, declaring, 'My father? The Sun is my father, and the earth is my mother, and on her bosom I will repose.'

Then the Shawnee chief addressed the council in his native language, which was translated with difficulty by the interpreter:

It is true that I am a Shawnee. My forefathers were warriors. Their son is a warrior. From them I only take my existence; from my tribe I take nothing. I am the maker of my own fortune: and, oh, that I could make that of my red people, and of my country, as great as the conceptions of my mind, when I think of the Spirit that rules the Universe! I would not then come to Governor Harrison, to ask him to tear up the treaty, and to obliterate the landmark; but I would say to him, 'Sir, you have liberty to return to your own country.'

The being within, communing with past ages, tells me, that once, nor until lately, there was no white man on this continent. That it then all belonged to red men, children of the same parents, placed on it by the Great Spirit that made them, to keep it, to traverse it, to enjoy its productions, and to fill it with the same race. Once a happy race. Since made miserable by the white race, who are never contented but always encroaching.

The way, and the only way, to check and stop this evil, is for all the red men to unite in claiming a common and equal right in the land, as it was at first, and should be yet; for it was never divided, but belongs to all, for the use of each. That no part has a right to sell, even to each other, much less to strangers; those who want all, and will not do with less. The white people have no right to take the land from the Indians, because they had it first; it is theirs. They may sell, but all must join. Any sale not made by all is not valid. The late sale is bad. It was made by a part only. Part do not know how to sell. It requires all to make a bargain for all. All red men have equal rights to the unoccupied land. The right of occupancy is as good in one place as in another. There cannot be two occupations in the same place. The first excludes all others. It is not so in hunting or travelling; for there the same ground will serve many; as they may follow each other all day; but the camp is stationary, and that is occupancy. It belongs to the first who sits down on his blanket or skins, which he has thrown upon the ground, and till he leaves it no other has a right.

As Tecumseh seated himself upon the ground once more, Harrison stood up and replied:

The white people when they arrived upon the continent, had found the Miamies in the occupation of all the country on the Wabash, and at that time the Shawanese were residents of Georgia from which they were driven by the Creeks. That the land had been purchased from the Miamies, who were the true and original owners of it. That it was ridiculous to assert that all the Indians were one nation, for if such had been the intention of the Great Spirit he would not have put six different tongues into their heads, but have taught them all to speak a language all could understand. That the Miamies found it for their interest to sell a part of their lands, and receive for them a further annuity, the benefit of which they had long experienced, from the punctuality with which the seventeen fires (U.S. states) complied with their engagements; and that the Shawanese had no right to come from a distant country and control the Miamies in the disposal of their own property.

(Harrison's *Memoirs*)

As the interpreter explained this, Tecumseh replied furiously: 'Sell a country! Why not sell the air, the clouds and the great sea as well as the earth? Did not the Great Spirit make them all for the use of his children?'

Harrison attempted to placate the Shawnee chief by referring to the 'uniform regard to justice' demonstrated towards the Indians by the Americans. At this Tecumseh leapt to his feet, his eyes blazing with anger, crying: 'It is all false! Tell him he lies!'

An official ordered a lieutenant to summon reinforcements, muttering, 'This fellow means mischief, you'd better bring up the guard.'

Tecumseh's warriors now picked up their war-clubs and gathered around their chief. Harrison, upon learning that he was being called a liar, drew his sword to defend his honour. He calmly told the Shawnee leader, 'that he was a bad man – that he would have no further talk with him – that he must now return to his camp, and take his departure from the settlements immediately'. Tecumseh led his warriors away, and bloodshed was avoided.

Lesson on a Bench
The following day, Tecumseh sent apologies for any affront, and asked that the council be reconvened. Harrison consented, but guarded the

Nineteenth century Shawnee moccasins decorated with green, beige and red silk ribbon.

subsequent meeting with two companies of militia. At this council Tecumseh seated himself beside Harrison on a bench. He denied ever having intended to attack the governor, and excused his conduct by explaining, according to Harrison's memoirs, that he had been ill-advised by two white men; possibly British representatives or political opponents of the Governor.

As he explained all this, Tecumseh shuffled along the bench, forcing Harrison to do the same. When the Governor asked Tecumseh whether he would prevent a survey of the land, the chief declared his intention to 'adhere to the old boundary.'

Chiefs from the Wyandot, Kickapoo, Potawatomi, Ottawa, and Winnebago tribes all stood up to voice their support; while Tecumseh forced Harrison further along the bench. The Governor informed the Indians that their words would be conveyed to the President, but that the treaty lands would be defended by the sword. Now Tecumseh pushed along the council bench until Harrison protested that he was about to be shoved off. Thus, Tecumseh explained, laughing, the American settlers were forcing the Indians from their lands.

The following day, Harrison attempted to conciliate Tecumseh by meeting him in his own camp. He explained that the President would probably not comply with the chief's wishes, and Tecumseh replied:

Well, as the great chief is to determine the matter, I hope the Great Spirit will put sense

27

enough into his head to induce him to direct you to give up this land. It is true, he is so far off, he will not be injured by the war. He may sit still in his town and drink his wine, while you and I will have to fight it out.

Before leaving Vincennes, Tecumseh insisted that he would wage war to defend his land, saying, 'nor will I give rest to my feet until I have united all the red men in the like resolution.'

Harrison addressed to the War Department Tecumseh's complaint 'that the Americans had driven them from the sea-coasts, and that they would shortly push them into the lakes, and that they were determined to make a stand where they were.' Harrison himself found Tecumseh's grievances 'sufficiently insolent and his pretensions arrogant.' He further illustrated his attitude six weeks later when he spoke of the Indian land of the Old Northwest:

Is one of the fairest portions of the globe to remain in a state of nature, the haunt of a few wretched savages, when it seems destined, by the Creator, to give support to a large population and to be the sea of civilisation, of science, and true religion?

Forging the Alliance

Tecumseh once more travelled the eastern Woodlands of America to reaffirm the unity of his confederacy. In November of 1810, he ventured into Canada and pleaded for support from the Ottawa, Sauk, Fox, Potawatomi, Winnebago and Menominee tribes.

Then, in July of 1811, some settlers were killed by Potawatomi Indians in Illinois. Harrison, seizing his chance to take the offensive, summoned Tecumseh to Vincennes once more. Harrison insisted that the Indians responsible for the murders were followers of Tenskwatawa, and demanded that they be turned over at once. Tecumseh refused, and set out with twenty-four warriors the next day, to summon the Southern tribes to the war he knew now to be imminent. Tenskwatawa was dispatched back to Prophet's Town with instructions to avoid premature conflict with the Americans.

Tecumseh now made an epic six-month tour of the eastern and south-eastern tribes, visiting the tribes living in Mississippi, Georgia, the Carolinas, Alabama, Florida and Arkansas. He found growing support among the young warriors, but faced vociferous opposition from the older chiefs, grown fat on their government annuities. Generally, he found his dream of confederacy ill-prepared for war. Nevertheless, he persisted, with magnificent displays of oratory, beseeching the tribes to support him.

In Florida, Tecumseh found great support among the Seminole, and gave their chiefs bundles of red-painted sticks. He directed that after he sent word to them, they should cast away one stick each day. When they

28

had disposed of all the markers, they would know that the time was right for a simultaneous attack against the Americans by all the tribes supporting Tecumseh. From this practice, the tribe gained the nick-name of Red Sticks in the Seminole Wars.

Converting the Creek

Travelling up to Alabama, Tecumseh urged the Creek to join his confederacy and take up arms with the Seminole. His visit had a lasting effect upon Creek culture; he introduced one of his sacred war dances to the tribe, which was eagerly adopted and renamed the 'Dance of the Lakes'. At a large Creek council, Tecumseh addressed the Indians with his customary passion and eloquence:

Where today are the Pequot? Where are the Narragansett, the Mohican, the Pokanoket, and many other once powerful tribes of our people? They have vanished before the avarice and oppression of the White Man, as snow before a summer sun.

Will we let ourselves be destroyed in our turn without a struggle, give up our homes, our country bequeathed to us by the Great Spirit, the graves of our dead and everything that is dear and sacred to us? I know you will cry with me, 'Never! Never!'

In October 1811, at Tukabatchi, a Creek town on the west bank of the

Shawnee water drum and drum-stick, used to accompany ceremonial and social dances. The drum's adornments identify it as belonging to the Hathawekela (Eagle) division of the Shawnee.

Tallapoosa River, a council of 5000 Indians heard Tecumseh's war-like rhetoric:

Accursed be the race that has seized on our country and made women of our warriors. Our fathers from their tombs reproach us as slaves and cowards. I hear them now on the wailing winds . . . the spirits of the mighty dead complain. Their tears drop from the wailing skies. Let the white race perish. They seize your land, they corrupt your women, they trample on the ashes of your dead. Back whence they came upon a trail of blood, they must be driven.

At the lodge of the influential Tukabatchi chief Menawa or Big Warrior, Tecumseh made another speech designed to fan the flames of Creek hatred towards the whites. Menawa feigned approval and Tecumseh presented him with a bundle of red sticks, a piece of wampum, and a tomahawk, to symbolise the Creek chief's allegiance to the Shawnee. Then, looking into Big Warrior's eyes, and reading his actual intentions, Tecumseh declared:

Your blood is white. You have taken my talk, and the sticks, and the wampum, and the hatchet, but you do not mean to fight. I know the reason. You do not believe the Great Spirit has sent me. You shall know. I leave Tukabatchi directly – and shall go straight to Detroit. When I arrive there, I will stamp on the ground with my foot, and shake down every house in Tukabatchi.

As Tecumseh departed, the followers of Big Warrior began to count with dread the days until they estimated the Shawnee chief would arrive in Detroit. On that fateful day, the famous earthquake of Madrid shook every house in Tukabatchi to the ground, and the Creek murmured in terror, 'Tecumseh has got to Detroit.' This extraordinary miracle, which was testified to by Big Warrior's followers, was tangible proof of Tecumseh's great powers of prophecy; and the Creeks hurriedly took up their rifles to support him.

Tecumseh continued north, trying to piece together his visionary union. One of his orations was witnessed by Captain Sam Dale, a Mississippi Indian fighter:

'His eyes burned with supernatural lustre, and his whole frame trembled with emotion. His voice resounded over the multitude – now sinking in low and musical whispers, now rising to the highest key, hurling out his words like a succession of thunderbolts . . . I have heard many great orators, but I never saw one with the vocal powers of Tecumseh.'

Ashes of Prophet's Town

In the fall of 1811, some Indians stole the horses of an army dispatch rider. Harrison saw this as an opportunity to assail Prophet's Town, and break the power of the Indians, which had been growing alarmingly. Encouraged by Tecumseh's absence, Harrison determined, 'that that part of the fabric which he considered complete will be demolished and even its foundations rooted up.' Raising a militia of some 1000 men, Harrison marched up the Wabash towards Prophet's Town. Tenskwata-wa's emissaries met him on 6th November, and asked to council the

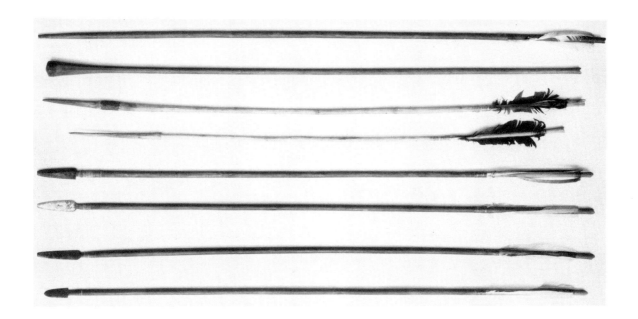

following day. Harrison agreed and camped on Burnet's Creek, three miles from the village. Fearing treachery, though, he wisely ordered his men to sleep in a circular formation, their guns beside them.

Tenskwatawa was distracted from his brother's warnings by the urging of a militant group of Winnebago warriors. He ordered an immediate attack, telling his followers that his medicine would make the white men as harmless as sand, and their bullets as soft as rain. Indeed, he proclaimed, many of the Americans were already dead. Crawling on their bellies, nearly 1000 Indian warriors advanced upon Harrison's camp before dawn.

At 3.45 a.m. on 7th November, 1811, a sentry spotted the warriors and discharged a shot before he was cut to the ground. The soldiers awoke to find bullets whistling amongst them, the Indians having broken their line in two places. Harrison master-minded a desperate defence until the Indians were driven off. The warriors mounted a series of furious charges throughout the night, but the inexperienced militia held firm, behaving, according to Harrison, 'in a manner that can never be too much applauded.' Harrison's commanding voice resounded above the noise of battle; meanwhile Tenskwatawa apparently skulked on a hill beyond the range of fire.

By dawn, the attacks had ceased. Sporadic fire continued throughout the day, but by nightfall the warriors had drifted silently away. Sixty-one soldiers had been killed, and twice as many wounded; Indian casualties were slightly lighter. On 8th November, Harrison found Prophet's Town abandoned, and burned it to the ground; along with Tecumseh's precious stores.

Tecumseh returned to Prophet's Town early in 1812, to find his

A collection of arrows from the Oklahoma Shawnee. The top one measures 31 inches.

brother and a diminished band of followers living among the ashes. Since Tenskwatawa had predicted that his medicine would assure an easy victory at the Battle of Tippecanoe, his credibility was now destroyed. Tecumseh was furious with him for having launched a premature attack. After shaking him by the hair and threatening to kill him, Tecumseh cast his brother into exile. With his religion discredited and without his brother's guidance, Tenskwatawa's influence quickly dwindled.

As Tecumseh had feared, the Indian tribes now sought vengeance independently, raiding the American settlements without Tecumseh to unify them. In despair, Tecumseh himself later recalled:

I stood upon the ashes of my own home . . . and there I summoned the spirits of the braves who had fallen in their vain attempt to protect their homes from the grasping invader, and as I snuffed up the smell of their blood from the ground I swore once more eternal hatred – the hatred of an avenger.

The War of 1812

As the Indian attacks spread panic among the settlements, American anger was directed increasingly at the British in Canada, whom the Americans believed to be fermenting Indian unrest. Border disputes and arguments over shipping rights also developed, and on 18th June 1812, the United States declared war on Great Britain.

Agents from both powers now sought the help of the Indians, and Tecumseh was unquestionably the most influential chief at this time. Quickly, he seized this last opportunity to unite the Indians, announcing to a large tribal council:

Here is a chance . . . a chance such as will never occur again: for us Indians of North America to form ourselves into one great combination and cast our lot with the British in this war. And should they conquer and again get the mastery of all North America, our rights to at least a portion of the land of our fathers would be respected by the King. If they should not win and the whole country should pass into the hands of the Long Knives – we see this plainly – it will not be many years before our last place of abode and our last hunting ground will be taken from us, and the remnants of the different tribes between the Mississippi, the Lakes, and the Ohio River will all be driven toward the setting sun.

Travelling to Fort Malden, Tecumseh pledged his support to the British. Attracted by his great name, and by the additional strength of his British allies, the Indian tribes at last came together into the confederacy he had conceived so many years before. Some tribes continued to attack the American settlements independently, but many rallied to Tecumseh's side. At Brownstown alone, American intelligence reported 1630 warriors drawn from the Shawnee, Winnebago, Kickapoo, Sauk, Potawatomi, Ottawa, Delaware, Seneca, and Ojibwa tribes. William Jones of the Indian Department recalled that 'as nearly as I can recollect there were about 10,000 souls, exclusive of children at the breast,' gathered in

At General Brock's side, Tecumseh leads the British forces into the captured city of Detroit, wearing a brigadier-general's scarlet overcoat and with Brock's own pistols in his sash.

scattered bands about the British posts. Many camped on Grosse Isle on the Detroit River, following Tecumseh.

'We are indebted . . . much more to the Chief Tecumthe for our Indian arm,' said Britain's Colonel Proctor. 'He convinced the Indians that our cause was theirs and his influence and example determined and fixed the Wyandots whose selection determined every tribe.' Later he remarked 'Tecumseh's example and talents governed the councils of his brethren.'

In recognition of those talents, the British gave Tecumseh independent command of the Indian forces, with the Indian Department providing advisers to the 2000 warriors. Tecumseh was given a regular commission as a brigadier general, an extraordinary rank to be attained by a tribal leader.

The wool bunting British flag said to have been given to Tecumseh when he was made a brigadier. The gift, from Sawa Banashe (Yellow Hawk), was then handed down as an heirloom.

Capture of Detroit

In July 1812, American General William Hull led 2200 men from Detroit to invade Canada. Hull had been a daring officer in the Revolution, but had grown nervous and, some said, senile. His ponderous advance was harried on both flanks by Tecumseh's Indians; slowly, he was forced to a halt.

Then on 4th August, Hull dispatched 200 men southward under Major Vanhorn. Their task was to meet and escort a supply convoy travelling under Captain Brush from the River Raisin. Tecumseh inter-

In his native deerskins, Tecumseh is shot down by Colonel Johnson's Kentuckian Cavalry while leading his Indians and faltering British troops in a last desperate charge at the Battle of the Thames, 5th October 1813.

cepted Vanhorn near Brownstown and his Indian warriors killed twenty soldiers. The rest were sent scurrying back to Hull but not before Tecumseh captured the American general's dispatches. Hull, alarmed at this break in his supply line, hurried back across the border to Detroit. This action only served to increase the troops' contempt for him. On 8th August, a new relief column of 600 men under Colonel Miller ventured south. In a bloody engagement at Monguaga, south of Detroit, they clashed with a large body of Indians led by Tecumseh and the famous Sauk chief Black Hawk. Tecumseh fought bravely, receiving a wound in the leg, but the Americans forced the Indians and their British allies to cross over into Canada once more.

On 13th August, 300 British reinforcements arrived at Fort Malden, Amherstburg, under Major General Isaac Brock. Brock was a pleasant but powerful officer, and Tecumseh and he quickly developed a close friendship and a mutual admiration. When Tecumseh suggested an immediate attack on Detroit, Brock, perceiving Hull's nervousness, agreed, overruling his own officers in the decision. Tecumseh demonstrated his detailed knowledge of the area by furnishing Brock with a hastily drawn map, etched on a piece of bark.

Brock said of Tecumseh, 'A more gallant warrior does not . . . exist,' and presented the Shawnee chief with an engraved compass, his pistols, and his officer's sash. When Brock saw Tecumseh the next day without the sash, he asked if he had displeased him. Tecumseh replied that, not wishing to wear such a mark of distinction when an older, more accomplished warrior was present, he had passed the sash on to his lieutenant the Wyandot chief Roundhead.

When Hull refused Brock's call for surrender, Tecumseh led his warriors across the river under the cover of the British guns. Hull had sent a new relief force south towards Brush's convoy, and Tecumseh quickly cut them off from Detroit. Brock meanwhile allowed a courier to be captured, who told Hull that 5000 Chippewa would shortly arrive to support the British. As Brock led 700 troops across the river, Tecumseh marched his 600 Indian warriors three times through a clearing, to convince the Americans that the Chippewa had arrived.

Hull was fooled. On 16th August, without consulting his officers, and with his men planning to mutiny in order to continue the fight, the frightened old commander raised the white flag. He surrendered to a force half the size of his own.

Tecumseh marched proudly into Detroit, wearing a red cap topped with a single white-tipped eagle-feather, blue breechcloth, red leggings fringed with buckskin, and buckskin moccasins. About his shoulders was the British dress-coat of his rank, and around his neck a silver medal.

Hindrance of Proctor

After the capture of Detroit, Tecumseh's followers ravaged the Old

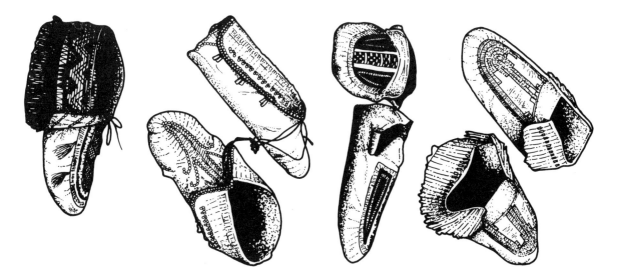

Northwest, capturing a number of American outposts. In the fall of 1812, Tecumseh found time to travel south again, and may have played some part in inciting the Creek War of 1813.

Brock had been killed in October 1812 and replaced by the far less able Colonel Henry Proctor, who would hinder Tecumseh's efforts constantly. General Harrison meanwhile took charge of the Second Northwestern Army, and led 1100 men north. On the Maumee River he built Fort Meigs, near the site of the Battle of Fallen Timbers. Tecumseh returned to Fort Malden in April, having instigated the mustering of some 4000 warriors, from the Shawnee, Sauk, Fox, Kickapoo, Winnebago, Menominee, Ojibwa, Wyandot, Delaware, Ottawa, Potawatomi, Miami and even the Sioux.

In April 1813, a British force of 2500 approached and besieged Fort Meigs under the command of Proctor and Tecumseh. When the fort held firm, Proctor chose to invest rather than storm it. His hesitancy, reminiscent of Hull, infuriated Tecumseh, and allowed the Americans to send for vital reinforcements.

On 5th May, some 1100 Kentuckians under General Greenclay emerged from the forests, taking the British completely by surprise. The militiamen in their eagerness broke ranks and charged into the British. The redcoats and Tecumseh's Indians made an incisive counter-attack, and surrounded the entire force. Nearly 500 of the Kentuckians were killed, and 150 captured.

While Tecumseh remained at the siege lines, the Kentuckian prisoners were marched down-river to Proctor's headquarters at Fort Miami. Here, twenty of them were tomahawked to death and scalped by the Indians in two hours of savage butchery. Proctor turned a blind eye, until Tecumseh suddenly arrived, his horse coated in sweat. Drawing his knife and tomahawk, Tecumseh plunged in to the Indian ranks and

Typical, highly-decorated, Woodlands skin moccasins, adorned with quillwork, beadwork, animal hair and metal cones. The Cree, who made moccasins from caribou and moose skin, estimated that each man used ten pairs a year.

35

Wampum *was woven into belts* (top) *to signify tribal authority and to represent treaty signings, both between tribes and with the whites. A predominantly dark purple belt symbolised sadness and death, and therefore probably a declaration of war. The ringed 'pouch' designs* (lower) *are less typical.*

brought the carnage to an immediate halt. Tearfully, he admonished, 'Oh, What will become of my Indians!'

Seeking out the Colonel, Tecumseh demanded to know why he had not prevented the slaughter. 'Sir,' Proctor replied, 'Your Indians cannot be commanded.'

With utter disdain, Tecumseh replied, 'Be gone! You are unfit to command; go and put on petticoats!'

Following an unsuccessful attempt to destroy Harrison's stores at nearby Fort Stephenson, Proctor grew weary of the campaining. In late July, he withdrew to Fort Malden on the Canadian side of the Detroit River, much to Tecumseh's disgust. Harrison was delighted, however, for it gave him precious time in which to build up a stronger army, which numbered 4500 men by September.

On 10th September 1813, the British Fleet on Lake Erie under Lieutenant Barclay was defeated by the American Navy led by Captain Perry. This cut the British supply line to Fort Malden, and – as Harrison prepared to march from Fort Meigs – left Proctor with no alternative but to retreat. For the next thirteen days, Proctor prepared for a retreat which he knew would be very unpopular among his Indian allies. Unfortunately, the timid commander did not have the courage to inform Tecumseh of the situation, and slyly concealed all plans for the retreat from the Indians for as long as possible.

On 13th September, Proctor ordered the dismantling of Fort Malden, to be executed quietly so as not to alarm the Indians! Tecumseh, whose rank alone gave him every right to be informed of Proctor's secret orders, inevitably discovered the commander's duplicity, and demanded that a council be held. On 18th September, the Indian chiefs gathered in the centre of Amherstburg council room. Around its walls stood the British officers, who declared their intention to retreat. In response,

A nineteenth century painting believed to be of Tecumseh.

36

Tecumseh stood up clutching a belt of wampum; and delivered a devastating speech. He concluded:

Father, listen! Our fleet has gone out, we know they have fought; we have heard the great guns; but know nothing of what has happened to our Father with one arm (Barclay). Our ships have gone one way, and we are much astonished to see our father tying up everything and preparing to run the other; without letting his red children know what his intentions are. You always told us to remain here and take care of our lands; it made our hearts glad to hear that was your wish. Our Great Father, the King, is the head and you represent him. You always told us that you would never draw your foot off British ground; but now, Father, we see you are drawing back, and we are sorry to see our Father doing so, without seeing the enemy. We must compare our Father's conduct to a fat animal that carries its tall, bushy tail upon its back; but when affrighted, it drops it between its legs and runs off.

While Tecumseh delivered his speech, one witness recalled, 'the darkness of his complexion and the brilliancy of his black and piercing eye, gave a singularly wild and terrific expression to his features. It was evident that he could be terrible.' There was muffled laughter at Proctor's expense as the interpreter translated Tecumseh's last sentence, before he continued:

Listen Father! The Americans have not yet defeated us by land; neither are we sure that they have done so by water; we therefore wish to remain here, and fight our enemy should they make their appearance. If they defeat us we will then retreat with our Father. At the battle of the Rapids (1794) the Americans certainly defeated us; and when we retreated to our Father's fort at that place the gates were shut against us. We were afraid that it would now be the case; but instead of that we now see our British Father preparing to march out of his garrison.

Father! You have got the arms and ammunition which our Great Father sent for his red children. If you have an idea of going away, give them to us, and you may go, and welcome for us. Our lives are in the hands of the Great Spirit. We are determined to defend our lands, and if it is his will, we wish to leave our bones upon them.

As Tecumseh finished, his chiefs leaped to their feet, screaming their approval. Proctor quickly left the council room, promising to make his reply in a subsequent council.

The following day, rumours abounded that the Indians planned to tear in two a belt of wampum at the next council, an act to symbolise the fracture of their alliance with the British. Proctor now summoned Tecumseh, and at last explained his reasons for retreating. Upon receiving assurances that the British would make a stand on the Thames, Tecumseh agreed to placate the other chiefs. Proctor affirmed his resolution to fight on the Thames at a second council later that day. Sending their guns and stores north-east up the Thames, the British withdrew to Sandwich on 23rd September. Burning all the buildings, they commenced the retreat up the Thames on 27th September.

Proctor's duplicity had cost Tecumseh some 800 followers; the Potawatomi Indians, in particular, drifting back to their villages. Tecumseh led about 1200 warriors up the Thames, reflecting to one of his comrades; 'We are now going to follow the British, and I feel certain that we shall never return.'

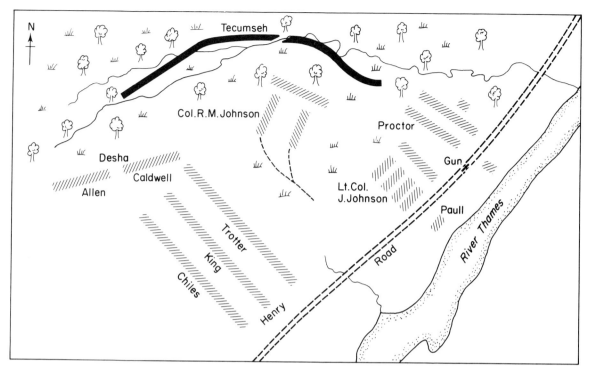

The map labels (as shown):

- N (compass)
- Tecumseh
- Col. R.M. Johnson
- Proctor
- Desha
- Caldwell
- Allen
- Lt. Col. J. Johnson
- Gun
- Paull
- Trotter
- King
- Chiles
- Henry
- Road
- River Thames

The deployment of the American, English and Indian troops at the Battle of the Thames, 5 October, 1813.

The Last Prophecy

Harrison led 2000 regulars and 3000 militia into Canada, and the smouldering remains of Fort Malden, on 27th September 1813. On 2nd October he proceeded with about 3500 men from Sandwich, in pursuit of the British. Tecumseh's Indians guarded Proctor's tail, and fought a furious rearguard action at MacGregor's Creek on 4th October. The battle lasted for two hours, but after being wounded in the arm, and losing thirteen warriors, Tecumseh was forced to retreat.

On the afternoon of 5th October 1813, the British and Indian army took up positions at Moraviantown, near present-day Chatham. Proctor seemingly remained reluctant to stand and fight, and Tecumseh was prominent in forcing the battle upon the British, and orchestrating their defences. The British arrayed their ranks on the north side of the Thames, with a swamp guarding their right flank. Tecumseh deployed his warriors in woodland to the north of the swamp; a larger marsh guarding their right flank.

Proctor's deficiencies had by now depleted the Indian forces, through disaffected desertion, to little more than 500 warriors. Tecumseh's choice of battlefield, though, was excellent. The forest would break up any cavalry charge, while the extent of the Indian lines would allow them to rake the Americans' left flank with fire.

Prior to the battle, Tecumseh and some British officers heard the sound of a shot, though none had been fired. Tecumseh doubled up momentarily as if hit, and told the officers that a bad spirit was present. He subsequently made his last prophecy, telling the chiefs that had remained loyal to his cause: 'Brother warriors, we are now about to enter into an engagement from which I shall never come out – my body will remain on the field of battle.'

He then offered his sword to one of them, saying, 'When my son becomes a noted warrior and able to wield a sword, give this to him.'

He dressed for the battle not in the scarlet coat of the British but in the deerskin of his people.

As the British forces awaited the Americans, Tecumseh instructed Proctor to re-deploy his men more sparsely, to minimise their exposure to enemy fire. He then reassured the general: 'Father! Have a big heart! Tell your young men to be firm and all will be well.'

Having thus raised Proctor's spirits, Tecumseh reviewed the troops. John Richardson, a volunteer in the British Forty-first Regiment of Foot recalled the event:

Only a few minutes before the clang of the American bugles was heard ringing through the forest . . . the haughty chieftain had passed along our line, pleased with the manner in which his left was supported, and seemingly sanguine of success. He was dressed in his usual deer skin dress, which admirably displayed his light yet sinewy figure, and in his handkerchief, rolled as a turban over his brow, was placed a handsome white ostrich feather, which had been given to him by a near relation of the writer . . . and on which he was ever fond of decorating himself, either for the Hall of Council or the battle field. He pressed the hand of each officer as he passed, made some remark in Shawnee, appropriate to the occasion, which was sufficiently understood by the expressive signs accompanying them, and then passed away forever from our view.

Another account, by Captain Hall, also provides a significant insight into the inspection and the demeanour of Tecumseh in contrast to that of Proctor:

After the line was formed I first me[t] General Proctor riding down from the right of the line towards the left with Colonel Elliot and Tecumseth. After they had passed the line and returned again, Colonel Elliot interpreted some observations that had passed between him and Tecumseth intended for the general. The first was that our men were too thickly posted – that they would be exposed to the enemy's riflemen, and thrown away to no advantage. The second was to desire his young men to be stout hearted as the enemy would make a push at the gun; Tecumseth then left the general apparently in very high spirits.

The impression is certainly created that the British and Indians alike took their inspiration not from Proctor, but from Tecumseh.

The Fatal Charge
Harrison's force of approximately 3000 men attacked at 4 p.m. on 5th October 1813. They were met by perhaps as few as 450 regulars and 500

The death of Tecumseh, at the Battle of the Thames, as shown in the painting by Alonzo Chappel, published in 1857.

Indians under the British flag. Harrison chose to mount a full-blooded cavalry charge into the British ranks. It was a measure which he conceded later was 'not sanctioned by anything I had seen or heard of; but I was fully convinced it would succeed.' Colonel Richard Johnson's Kentuckian cavalry made the charge, sending about 500 troopers against the British lines, and a like number across the swamp towards the Indians.

The charge broke the British lines almost immediately. The redcoats wounded only three or four American troops with their first volley. They did not even pause to reload before making a retreat described by one British officer as 'shameful in the highest degree.' Proctor fled to his carriage and galloped to the safety of eastern Ontario.

The Indians, in stark contrast, fought magnificently under Tecumseh's brave example. They unleashed a volley of fire which stopped the American cavalry charge in its tracks. The troopers were thrown back, and forced to dismount before entering the mêlée once more. The Indians met them in furious hand-to-hand fighting, Tecumseh at their centre, blood streaming down his face from a head wound, his arm still bandaged.

'He yelled like a tiger, and urged his braves to attack,' one American later recalled. Defiantly, Tecumseh led a charge into the heart of the American ranks. A bullet struck him in the left breast, and he fell, mortally wounded. His dream of an Indian confederacy fell with him in the dust of Moraviantown.

There is strong evidence to suggest that it was Johnson himself who killed Tecumseh. Some time later, William Clark, Superintendent of Indian Affairs at St. Louis questioned a Potawatami chief as to his memory of the events:

Were you at the battle of the Thames? Yes. Did you know Tecumseh? Yes. Were you near him in the fight? Yes. Did you see him fall? Yes. Who shot him? Don't know. Did you see the man that shot him? Yes. What sort of looking man was he? Short, thick man. What color was the horse he rode? Most white. How do you know this man shot Tecumseh? I saw the man ride up – saw his horse get tangled in some bushes – when the horse was most still, I saw Tecumseh level his rifle at the man and shoot – the man shook on his horse – soon the horse got out of the bushes, and the man spurred him up – horse came slow – Tecumseh right before him – man's left hand hung down – just as he got near, Tecumseh lifted his tomahawk and was going to throw it, when the man shot him with a short gun – Tecumseh fell dead and we all ran.

Demoralized by the British rout, and disheartened by the fall of their great prophet and chief, the Indians slowly gave way. They retreated to Moraviantown, and the battle was over.

Legacy and Legend

'With deep concern I mention the death of the chief Tecumthée, who was shot on the 5th instant.' So read Proctor's despatch of 23rd October 1813, but the facts surrounding Tecumseh's demise were far less simple.

Native dress of a Shawnee man, and probably not unlike that of Tecumseh prior to his adoption of European uniform of around 1796. Note the roach haircut, (red) face paint, ear ornaments, bead necklace, cloth shirt and breechcloth, white blanket, cloth leggings, garters, silver armlet with feather pendants, and bow with fletched arrows.

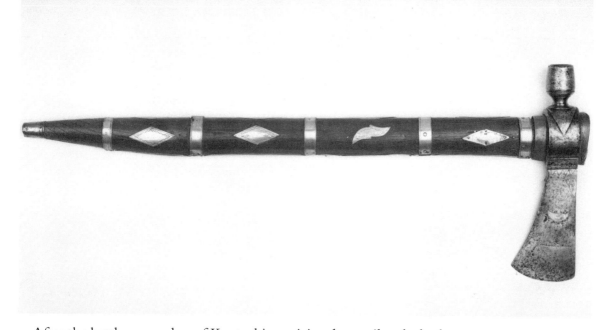

A fine example of a Shawnee pipe-tomahawk, from the Bragge Collection, showing the silver decoration on the shaft.

After the battle, a number of Kentuckians viciously mutilated a body identified, by British officers amongst others, as being that of Tecumseh. They scalped the corpse, and tore long strips of skin from its back and thighs. The body subsequently disappeared, and was secretly interred by the Indians. Tecumseh's followers later claimed that this was not in fact the body of the Shawnee chief. Tecumseh's body, they insisted, had been carried away by his followers immediately after the battle, and buried in an unknown place.

For years, the Americans were plagued by rumours that Tecumseh was in fact still alive. These were unquestionably false, but reflected the fear and respect in which Tecumseh was held. Despite claims to various graves, the site of his resting place remains an intriguing mystery. One set of bones was preserved on St. Annes Island by the Indian chief Sha-wah-wan-noo, and found its way eventually to Walpole Island. Here, a monument to Tecumseh was raised over them, in 1941; despite the fact that the thigh-bones did not demonstrate the fractures suffered by Tecumseh as a young man.

The decline of the Indian alliance with the British was inevitably accelerated by Tecumseh's death. Without a leader of his strength, the British found those Indians that remained loyal, impossible to control. Naibush, the Ottawa chief, described the disunity:

Since our great chief Tecumtha has been killed, we do not listen to one another, we do not rise together, we hurt ourselves by it, it is our own fault . . . we do not when we go to war rise together, but we go one or two and the rest say they will go tomorrow.

Tecumseh's immediate followers turned to Tenskwatawa for leadership, and raised Tecumseh's son Puchethei, to the status of village chief, in honour of his father. They settled for a time at Fort Malden at the mouth of the Detroit River.

When the Americans signed the peace treaty at Ghent on 24th December 1814, they refused to concede British demands for a separate Indian state. Without a leader of Tecumseh's stature, the disordered Shawnee tribes, like all the fragmented tribes of the Old Northwest, were forced westward by American settlement. The various Shawnee divisions eventually settled in three distinct groups in Oklahoma.

Tecumseh's legend was powerful enough to enhance subsequent presidential elections. In 1837, Richard Johnson, the man most championed as the actual slayer of the Shawnee chief, ran for election with the slogan: 'Rumpsey, Dumpsey, Colonel Johnson killed Tecumseh.' Three years later, Harrison, with running mate John Tyler, succeeded to the White House using the nick-name he had acquired by destroying Prophet's Town: 'Tippecanoe and Tyler too.'

Though his dreams of an Indian state, and a grand confederacy of tribes, died at the Battle of the Thames, Tecumseh continued to be remembered as 'a saint' by the Shawnee. When Catlin met Tenskwatawa in 1830, the fallen Prophet said of his brother 'Tecumseh was a great general, and that nothing but his premature death defeated his grand plan'.

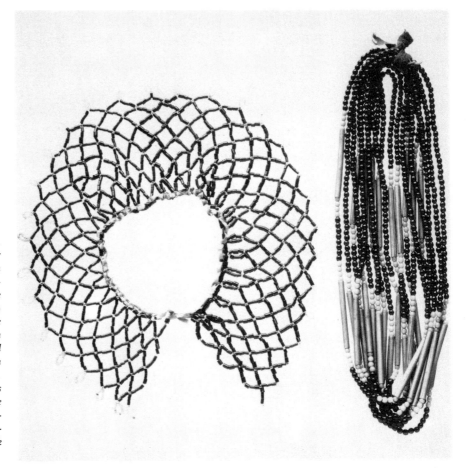

By the mid-nineteenth century, the Shawnee, like many of their former neighbours, ended up in Oklahoma as a result of government land cedes. This Shawnee man and small boy (opposite) were photographed there around 1900 – a long way in time and culture from the proud days of their ancestors in Tecumseh's Old Northwest. Nevertheless, traditional crafts still flourished among the Shawnee even after their relocation to Oklahoma as evidenced by this fine beadwork collar and necklace.

Chronology of Events

1675–76	War of King Philip (Metacom).
1754–63	French and Indian War.
1763	Royal Proclamation prohibits settlement west of Appalachians.
1763–4	Pontiac's Rebellion.
1768	MARCH Tecumseh born at Piqua, on Mad River.
1774	Thirteen Mingoes and Shawnee murdered by settlers.
1774	Lord Dunmore's War.
	6 October: Battle of Point Pleasant.
	NOVEMBER: Cornstalk signs treaty with Lord Dunmore at Chillicothe.
1775–83	American Revolution.
1777	Cornstalk murdered.
1778	General Edward Hand destroys Shawnee villages.
1778	Shawnee capture Daniel Boone.
1780	Major George Rogers Clark destroys Chillicothe and Piqua settlements.
1783	Tecumseh flees from Mad River battle.
	Treaty of Paris.
	Indian council on the Sandusky.
1788	Tecumseh breaks a leg, falling from his horse.
	Tecumseh travels among Missouri and Illinois Shawnee, Miami, Kickapoo, Creek and Cherokee.
	Cheesekau killed.
1790	SEPTEMBER: General Harmar defeated by Little Turtle.
1791	NOVEMBER: General St. Clair defeated by Little Turtle.
1793	Sandusky conference.
1794	AUGUST: Battle of Fallen Timbers.

1795	Greenville Treaty.
1796	Tecumseh marries half-breed Manete. His son Puchethei is born.
1799	Tecumseh meets Rebecca Galloway.
1800	Indiana Territory created.
1805	Laulewasika receives vision, and becomes Tenskwatawa, the Prophet.
	16 JUNE Tenskwatawa performs eclipse miracle.
	Tecumseh forms alliance with the Wyandot Roundhead.
1808	Prophet's Town established.
1808	Tecumseh travels among tribes from Missouri down to Florida.
1809	Treaty of Fort Wayne.
1810	AUGUST: Tecumseh meets Governor Harrison at Vincennes.
1811	JULY: Settlers killed by Potawatomi Indians.
	Tecumseh visits eastern and south-eastern tribes.
	OCTOBER: Tecumseh predicts earthquake.
	NOVEMBER: Battle of Tippecanoe. Harrison destroys Prophet's Town.
1812	Tecumseh exiles Tenskwatawa.
1812–15	War of 1812.
	AUGUST: Tecumseh and General Brock capture Detroit.
	AUTUMN: Tecumseh visits Creek.
	APRIL: Tecumseh and General Proctor besiege Fort Meigs.
1813	SEPTEMBER: British fleet defeated on Lake Erie. Proctor retreats.
	5 OCTOBER: Tecumseh killed in Battle of the Thames (Moraviantown).

Bibliography

Brandon, W. *American Heritage Book of Indians* American Heritage, 1982.

Catlin, G. *North American Indians* Dover, 1973.

Drake, B. *Life of Tecumseh and his brother the Prophet* Cincinnati, 1841.

Drake, S.G. *The Book of the Indians of North America* Boston, 1836.

Embleton, R. *Pioneers and Heroes of the Wild West* Parnell 1979.

Hodge, F.W. *Handbook of American Indians* Rowman and Littlefield, 1979.

Howard, J.H. *Shawnee!* Ohio University Press, 1981.

Josephy, A.M. *The Patriot Chiefs* Viking, 1961.

McKenney and Hall *History of the Indian Tribes of North America* Edinburgh, 1933.

Mcluhan, T.C. *Touch The Earth* Abacus, 1971.

Sturtevant, W.C. *Handbook of North American Indians – Northeast* Smithsonian Institution, 1978.

Sugden, J. *Tecumseh's Last Stand* Oklahoma University Press, 1985.

Swanton, J.R. *The Indian Tribes of North America* Oklahoma University Press, 1985.

Tucker, G. *Tecumseh, Vision of Glory* Indianapolis, 1956.

Utley, R.M. *The Indian Wars* Mitchell Beazley, 1977.

Waldman, C. *Atlas of the North American Indian* Facts on File, 1985.

Index

Page numbers in *italics* refer to illustrations.